A Submariner's Tale

A Submariner's Tale

ANDREW BUTTERFIELD

Story Terrace

Text Paddy Magrane, on behalf of StoryTerrace
Copyright © Andrew Butterfield

First print July 2024

This book is dedicated to my sons – Daniel, who died tragically aged 34, on 1st December 2022, and Lewis, who is my backbone – and to my grandchildren, Libby, Shaye, Grace, Millie, Grayson and Ronnie. I hope from this book they understand who I am and what I did for my Queen and country.

CONTENTS

1. EARLY MORNINGS AND THE MILKMAN

I was born on 11th August 1961 at Morecambe Hospital, the newest addition to a family that fully embraced the party atmosphere of the swinging '60s. My parents, along with their entire street in Heysham, Lancashire, where we lived, threw themselves into the hedonistic lifestyle of the decade. As a toddler, I grew accustomed to the sounds of laughter and clinking glasses echoing through our home well into the early morning hours.

I discovered a penchant for early-morning adventures when I was about four years old. With my mother and father still fast asleep, recovering from the previous night's revelry, I would escape from my bedroom window and embark on solitary explorations of the world beyond our bungalow. The crisp morning air filled my lungs as I wandered through the garden, climbing the sturdy branches of our apple tree to watch the birds flit among the leaves, enjoying their song and the peace.

One particularly memorable morning, as I was perched in the apple tree and the sun began to peek over the horizon, I spotted the milkman approaching our house in his electric float, bottles clinking in the rear. When he spotted me, he struck up a conversation. He explained what he did and offered me the chance to ride along with him on his rounds.

The milkman, whose name escapes me now, was a lovely man who wanted to give a curious child a bit of fun and adventure.

And so, at the tender age of four, I began accompanying the milkman on his daily rounds. Every morning, between six and seven o'clock, he would collect me from outside my bungalow and whisk me away on a journey through the sleeping streets of Heysham. For an hour each day, I rode alongside him in his float, watching as he delivered milk to the doorsteps of our slumbering neighbours. It was a magical time for me, a chance to see the world from a new perspective and to form a special bond with a kind and generous man.

The milkman always made sure that I had a bottle of milk of my own to take home, a small reward for my assistance on his rounds. It was a gesture that meant the world to me, a little boy who didn't always feel appreciated or loved at home.

My father, a man of old-school values, ruled our household with an iron fist. He was a hard man, not given to shows of affection or praise. My mother, timid and cowed by his domineering presence, rarely spoke unless spoken to. She loved me, but my father's resentment of me only grew stronger as I got older, peaking when I eventually rose through the ranks in the Navy and exceeded anything he had achieved during his own time as a conscript.

As I grew older, my responsibilities extended beyond my personal growth and adventures. When I was around seven or eight, my father's cousin and his daughter, Lynden, moved into a house next door. Just a month younger than me, Lynden quickly became essential to my life. I took on the role of protector and guardian, looking out for her as if she were my little sister.

One freezing winter morning, I went to the front room and found Lynden shivering and complaining about the chill in the air. Determined to keep her warm, I set out to light the gas fire in the living room. It was a very bad idea, in hindsight. With a roll of newspaper and some matches, I attempted to ignite the flames, but my inexperience led to disaster. As I rushed to transfer the burning paper to the gas fireplace, the flames licked at my fingers, causing me to drop the smouldering bundle into a nearby wicker basket.

The basket erupted into flames in an instant, and the contents spilled onto me. Clothing melted against my skin, searing my face and left arm. The pain was excruciating, and I could feel the heat blistering my flesh. Panic set in as I realised the gravity of the situation—not only was I in agony, but the fire threatened to engulf the entire room.

I sprang into action, ignoring the excruciating pain as I grabbed the flaming basket and hurled it away from Lynden. I found a bucket and filled it with water, frantically trying to douse the flames before they could spread further. 'What are you doing?' my mother called out, alerted by the commotion.

'I'm putting the fire out!' I yelled back, dumping another bucket of water onto the smouldering sofa where the basket had landed.

In the aftermath, as the smoke cleared and the immediate crisis had been averted, I caught a glimpse of myself in the mirror. My face and arm were a mess of reddened skin and painful blisters. I looked like something out of a horror film!

But even through the pain, I could only think about whether Lynden was OK. I had managed to protect her from the worst of it, and that was the most important thing.

My father, true to form, offered no sympathy for my injuries or praise for my quick thinking. Instead, he told me off for causing the fire in the first place. It was just another example of how I could never seem to do anything right in his eyes. His disapproval and lack of affection would shape my teenage years and, to some extent, the rest of my life. But I took solace in the fact that I had kept Lynden safe. No matter what my father thought of me, I knew that I had done the right thing.

The fire incident marked a turning point in my young life. It was the moment when I began to understand the weight of responsibility and the importance of looking out for those who needed protection. This lesson would serve me well in the years to come as I navigated the challenges of school, the Navy and, crucially, being an officer among its ranks. But it was also a stark reminder of the lack of warmth and support I received at home.

Despite the challenges at home, I found solace in my friendship with Lynden and in my early morning adventures with the milkman. Those stolen moments of freedom and companionship were a lifeline for me, a glimpse of a world beyond the confines of my complicated family life. They gave me the strength and resilience I would need to face the trials and tribulations that lay ahead.

My friend Henry the milkman took me on his round for for two years from age 4 to 6.
My reward a pint of milk a day.

2. SCHOOLYARD SCRAPES AND LIFELONG LESSONS

Entering Sandylands Primary School in Heysham was like stepping into an entirely new world. The school became my playground and battlefield. It was the 1960s, an era marked by significant societal changes, and the school environment reflected the time's dynamic nature. I quickly adapted to this new environment, finding excitement in the challenges and opportunities that came my way.

From the outset, it was evident that I had a natural aptitude for learning. Academic work came easily to me, and I often excelled in subjects like maths and history without putting in that much effort. My teachers quickly noticed my abilities, marking me out as a student with great potential. The structured school environment starkly contrasted with my often chaotic home life, and I thrived under the guidance of my teachers, where I felt the security of boundaries.

My emergence as a leader among my peers complemented my academic prowess. I formed a close-knit group of about six friends who looked up to me for guidance and protection. We were a gang in the most innocent sense of the word, sharing adventures and sticking up for each other. If there was a dispute on the playground, I stepped in and resolved it. And if someone needed defending, I was there to stand up for them, with my fists, if necessary. These early leadership experiences and camaraderie shaped my character and taught me the importance of loyalty and courage.

One of the more light-hearted aspects of school life involved the typical childhood antics that took place behind the bike shed, where my friends and I experienced our first awkward kisses. These innocent moments of exploration were a rite of passage, part of the growing-up process.

But as we grew older, the dynamics shifted. My success in school began to attract attention, and not all of it was positive. Some peers envied my achievements, and I sensed a growing resentment. However, I refused to let this deter me. I was confident in my abilities and determined to make the most of my potential.

Among the many teachers who influenced my early education, Mr Hurst stood out. He was my teacher in the fifth year and one of the best educators I have ever encountered. Nearing retirement, Mr Hurst was a seasoned teacher with a passion for his work and a genuine interest in his students. He had a unique ability to connect with each student, understanding their individual needs and helping them achieve their best. His kindness and patience balanced his strictness (he wasn't afraid to use the cane), and he significantly impacted my development.

Mr Hurst introduced me to two activities that would profoundly influence my life: chess and swimming. Chess appealed to my love of strategic thinking and problem-solving. I spent countless hours learning the game, mastering the rules and developing strategies. This early exposure to the game taught me to think several moves ahead and to anticipate the actions of others, skills that would prove invaluable in many areas of my life, not least the Navy, where we were often having to second-guess the Soviets!

Swimming, however, had an even more profound effect on me. Mr Hurst took a special interest in teaching three of us— John Rushton, John Pearson and myself—how to swim. Under his guidance, we worked diligently, progressing through the various swimming medal groups. Our dedication paid off when we became the first three students from our school to earn gold medal awards in swimming. This achievement was celebrated in the local newspapers, and my mother was thrilled. Needless to say, my father was unmoved by my achievement, which was really hurtful, but the overall sense of accomplishment and the recognition we received were exhilarating.

More than just a physical skill, swimming awakened in me a deep love for the sea. The countless hours spent in the water, pushing myself to improve, began to shape my true passion, if only at an unconscious level. I think I realised, even though I could not yet articulate it, that the sea was where I belonged, and this discovery would shape my future in ways I couldn't have imagined at the time. Swimming taught me discipline, perseverance and the joy of pursuing something I loved.

Sadly, at home, life was not so clear-cut. My father continued to rule our household with his iron fist. As I grew older, my relationship with him became more and more strained. My mother, timid and submissive, rarely spoke up against him. She loved me in her quiet way, but my father's dominance overshadowed her. My efforts to impress him—such as the swimming medal—all too often went unnoticed or were met with harsh criticism. His favouritism towards my younger sister Susan, who was four years my junior, was evident, and I frequently felt like an outsider in my own family.

As I prepared to transition from primary to secondary school, I carried with me the lessons and experiences of my early years. Sandylands Primary School provided a solid foundation of knowledge and a sense of confidence in my abilities. My achievements in swimming and chess, along with the lessons I'd learned from Mr Hurst, had shaped my character and prepared me for the next stage of my education.

Despite my father's lack of support, I was determined to forge my own path. I excelled in my 11-plus exams, achieving top marks in several subjects. My academic success was my way of proving my worth, but it did little to change my father's perception of me. Nevertheless, I refused to be defined by his disapproval. I had developed a strong sense of self-worth and determination, and I was resolved to make the most of the opportunities that lay ahead.

As I prepared for secondary school, I began to think about where my life would take me as an adult. I had long assumed I would join my father's washing machine rent-and-repair business or follow his wishes, and join the Merchant Navy. But it began to dawn on me that his suggestion was only about ensuring I left home and never returned. He simply didn't want me around.

The decision—which I came to much later in my adolescence—to join the Royal Navy was a significant turning point in my life. It represented a break from my father's expectations and a step towards forging my own path. The lessons I had learned at school, both in the classroom and in the schoolyard, had prepared me for the next phase in my life. But first came secondary school, and more adventures—and misadventures.

A selection of pictures showing my growing up from Tot to Teen.

3. BITTER BETRAYAL AND A
TIME TO ESCAPE

As I strode through the imposing double doors of Balmoral School (later renamed Heysham High and now known as the Bay Leadership Academy), I was carrying a weighty reputation as a fighter. It was a label I had earned through countless scrapes and scuffles at primary school, a badge of honour in the rough-and-tumble world of my youth. But on that crisp autumn morning, as the sunlight streamed through the colourful leaves, I was determined to shed that old identity and carve out a new path for myself.

But while a fresh start beckoned, I knew that I would first have to prove myself, so I could cement my reputation before putting it to bed once and for all.

And so, on that first day, I sought out the biggest, toughest lad in the school and challenged him to a fight. It was a brutal affair, a clash of wills and fists that left us both battered and bruised. But in the end, I emerged victorious, and with that single act of defiance, I established myself as a force to be reckoned with.

Following that day, a palpable aura of respect and fear surrounded me at school. No one dared to challenge me, and I had solidified my place in the school's hierarchy. I finally felt a sense of belonging and no longer had to engage in physical battles.

Life outside school was a mix. At weekends, I earned 50p an hour calling numbers in my cousin's bingo hall by the sea. At home, my father's chilling indifference and casual cruelty seemed to intensify with each passing day, leaving me yearning for warmth and kindness that seemed increasingly out of reach.

Whatever the reason, I found myself increasingly drawn to the freedom and adventure of the open sea. It was a siren call that tugged at my heart, a whisper of something greater than the life I had known thus far.

An episode when I was about 11 confirmed what was building in me. One morning, as I sat on the sandpit by the long jump at school, minding my own business, a bottle came flying out of nowhere and struck me on the top of the head. The impact was devastating, leaving me concussed and bleeding profusely.

As I lay there, dazed and in agony, the school called my father to come and fetch me. But instead of rushing to my aid, he took his sweet time, arriving an hour later with an air of irritation and inconvenience. And rather than taking me straight to the hospital, he insisted on dragging me to the Yacht Club first, where he had some business to attend to.

I sat there, a towel pressed to my bleeding head, sipping an orange juice, while my father chatted and drank with his friends. It was an act of supreme indifference, a surreal and horrifying experience that crystallised in me the depth of his callousness and neglect.

By the time he finally decided to take me to the hospital, I had already passed out from blood loss. I woke up hours later with a number of stitches in my head and a grim realisation settling over me like a shroud. I'd long suspected it, but the day's grim events had confirmed it. My father simply didn't care about me. His neglect had nearly cost me my life, and I knew at that moment that I had to get away.

But escaping wasn't as easy as just walking out the door. I still had school to contend with, and despite my growing disillusionment, I found solace in the mental challenges of the classroom. Chess, in particular, continued to be a passion of mine.

I challenged the top player in the school league and quickly established myself as a formidable opponent. For the rest of my school days, I remained at the top, honing my skills and learning to think in both short-term and long-term strategies. It was a valuable lesson, one that would serve me well in the years to come.

But even as I excelled in chess, I found myself growing more and more restless with the confines of the classroom.

During these years, one of my closest friends was Andy Anderson, known to me simply as Andy. We became best friends around the third year of secondary school. Andy was not particularly interested in academia. Instead, he was more focused on enjoying life and pushing the boundaries of what was allowed. It was Andy who introduced me to the concept of skiving off school and in the fourth and fifth years, he and I began bunking off for entire days at a time.

It was a simple enough scheme. We would sign the register in the morning, then duck out and spend the day hiding out at my house or Andy's. My parents were out most of the day, so it was easy enough to avoid detection. And for a while, it seemed like the school didn't even notice we were missing.

But, of course, all good things must come to an end. One day, as I was trying to slip out down the main drive, I ran smack into the headmaster himself. My card was immediately marked. I tried to bluff my way out of it, claiming it was break time and I was on my way to a dentist appointment. But unsurprisingly, he wasn't having it.

He marched me straight to the geology class I was supposed to be in, only for the teacher to declare that she had never seen me before! I'd never attended her class, and was well and truly scuppered. The consequences were severe.

My father was called in, and when he found out what I had been up to, he flew into a rage. He gave me a hard thrashing, leaving me badly bruised. It was a brutal and very painful reminder of the man he was, and the life I so desperately wanted to escape.

Even through the pain and humiliation, I steadfastly refused to let my father's abuse define me. I channelled my energy and natural intelligence into achieving success, managing to pass my O-Levels and CSEs without once returning to school or engaging in extensive revision. This accomplishment acted as a testament to my resilience and determination to overcome adversity.

During this challenging time, a compelling plan began to take shape in my mind. My close friend Andy had recently joined the Navy, and he was particularly enthusiastic about the Submarine Service.

Andy's firsthand experiences, from undergoing interviews to touring a submarine, left him brimming with excitement about the strong camaraderie and gripping adventures that awaited him in the Submarine Service. His enthusiasm sparked a fire in me, igniting a desire to embark on a new and promising path filled with camaraderie and thrilling adventures.

I was captivated by the idea and decided to visit the recruitment office to delve deeper into this opportunity. As I learned more, I felt a profound connection stirring within me. It was as if I had finally found my true calling, a sense of belonging that had eluded me for so long.

Embarking on the recruitment process, I encountered a series of rigorous interviews in Preston and Liverpool. These challenges only fuelled my determination to succeed, pushing me to prove that I was capable of rising above my reputation as a rebellious teenager with a chip on his shoulder. It became a personal mission to demonstrate to myself and others that I held the potential for something greater.

But even as I pursued my dreams, the spectre of trauma reared its ugly head once again. After my second interview in Liverpool, I went to a pub to celebrate. There, I was befriended by a man who plied me with cigarettes and offered to take me to the station.

But instead of the station, he walked me to a car park, where he overpowered me and brutally raped me. It was a shattering, deeply upsetting experience, one that left me reeling with shock and pain. But even in that moment of despair, I found the strength to fight back. As he tried to bundle me into a cab that I believe was destined for his house, I kicked my attacker in the bollocks and ran, leaving him writhing on the ground behind me.

It was an experience that, until now, I have never spoken of —a secret shame that I buried deep inside myself that day as I focused instead on my plans to join the Navy. And when I finally got the chance to visit a submarine being built in a dry dock in Barrow-in-Furness, I knew beyond a shadow of a doubt that I had made the right choice.

On 30th August 1977, just 19 days after celebrating my 16th birthday, I took a significant step in my life by enlisting in the Royal Navy. This decision marked the beginning of a new and transformative chapter in my life, one that would lead me away from the hardships and disappointments of my earlier years and into a world of excitement and purpose.

Basic training at HMS Raleigh in Plymouth was a wake-up call for me. The abrupt transition to service life brought with it a very short haircut, rigorous drills and a level of discipline that was entirely new to me. However, I embraced the challenge wholeheartedly, pouring my determination into every aspect of my training to prove myself worthy of the uniform I now proudly wore.

I was placed in Cunningham Division, living in a barrack room of around 20 beds with my peers. In all exercises, we competed against other divisions and were identified by Cunningham's divisional colour—yellow.

For six weeks, I dedicated myself to the intense regimen of basic training—marching, classroom learning, assault courses and meticulously maintaining every aspect of my uniform, which meant shining boots until they gleamed like a mirror. The experience taught me the immeasurable value of teamwork, camaraderie and discipline as I forged enduring connections with my fellow recruits.

I remember one unsettling episode. The division had been out at the pub and we returned to the barrack room to find two cadets having sex. Homosexuality was strictly forbidden in the Navy, which meant we had to report what we had witnessed. But the punishment that was meted out seemed unusually harsh.

They were marched outside and forced to stand naked in the bitterly cold wintry weather for hours. The next morning, they were gone, never to be seen again. They'd been dismissed, their naval careers abruptly over. It was a sad moment in an otherwise happy period.

The pride I felt when I graduated with the title Junior Seaman, with my beaming mother in the audience, was unparalleled—it was a moment of profound accomplishment and fulfilment, although I don't remember my father attending.

But HMS Raleigh wasn't finished with me yet. The next stage was warfare training, which consisted of another six weeks, this time focused on classroom learning and exercises like knot tying. Much of it had very little to do with warfare. Instead, it was focused on bonding teams.

I welcomed the new challenges with open arms, viewing them as an opportunity to once again prove my mettle and secure my position among the esteemed ranks of the Submarine Service. When the six weeks were complete, I passed out again, to my delight.

The bitter experiences and betrayals of my past were behind me now, and a new world of opportunity and adventure beckoned. I bid farewell to HMS Raleigh, ready for the even tougher challenges of submarine training.

Friends for life

Betrayed by a shipmate and punished by the Captain. I got 14 Days punishment
working 20 hours a day scrubbing toilets.

4. PUSHING MY LIMITS

Once I stepped through the gates of Fort Blockhouse at HMS Dolphin in Gosport, a wave of anticipation and trepidation washed over me. This was the beginning of my journey to becoming a true submariner, where I would be tested in ways I had never experienced before. The challenge was daunting, but I was ready and eager to prove myself and earn my place among the elite ranks.

The first major hurdle was the infamous Submarine Escape Training, a rite of passage for every aspiring submariner. At the heart of this was the Submarine Escape Training Tank (SETT), a 100-foot (30-metre) deep facility primarily operated to conduct training with submarine escape equipment, which was operated by the Royal Navy. The facility incorporated a fresh, chlorinated water column with a single escape chamber (in common with all classes of Royal Navy submarines) mounted at the base, through which students had to conduct a fully representative escape cycle from 100 feet (30 m), closely replicating actions which would be required if forced to abandon a distressed submarine from depth. The SETT has its own dedicated boiler house to maintain its water temperature at 34°C (94°F). The SETT was commissioned in 1954, with the first students trained in July of that year. Since that time completion of 'the Tank' has

been obligatory for all Royal Navy Submariners. Training included ascents from increasing depths as a major element, but in addition, it was underpinned by lectures and practical training in how to survive within a disabled submarine, operation of emergency equipment and survival techniques on reaching the surface—a package
of potentially life-saving skills.

Over the years, the SETT has been used to train submariners from Italy, the US, Greece, Canada, Israel, Russia, Venezuela, Turkey, Australia and the Netherlands— with the staff and facility enjoying a worldwide reputation for excellence and good practice. Owing to a combination of increased safety associated with modern submarine design, submarines operating in areas where escape would be impossible with current equipment and the risks associated with the conduct of training, the Navy discontinued pressurised submarine escape training in March 2009. It was the end of an era!

As an aside, the staff at SETT were drawn from the ranks of the UK Submarine Service. All members of SETT staff formed part of the SMERAT (Submarine Escape and Rescue Advisory Team), some members formed the UK SPAG (Submarine Parachute Assistance Group), and others formed part of the UK contribution to the NSRS (LR5) Team. All staff were trained in advanced life-saving techniques and diving medicine.

The SETT was a gruelling test of physical and mental endurance designed to push us beyond our absolute limits. Every man who aspired to join the submarine service had to pass this test. It was a cornerstone of our training, separating those who could handle the pressures of underwater life from those who could not.

That massive water tower loomed over us like a constant reminder of the dangers we would face in the depths of the ocean. The tower was a stark, cylindrical monolith, its sheer size intimidating to even the most confident among us. Inside, the water was dark, a silent testament to the challenges ahead. But I was determined to conquer it, mastering the skills that would keep me alive in the most extreme circumstances.

Submarine escape training is a complex interplay of physics and physiology. The pressure increases by one atmosphere, or 10 BAR, for every 30 feet of depth. This concept, though simple enough to grasp in the classroom, becomes a scary reality when experienced firsthand. The sensation of increasing pressure as you descend is almost indescribable. It's as if the weight of the ocean is pressing down on you, squeezing your body from all sides.

Our training began with simulated escapes from 30 feet, progressing to 60 feet, and finally, the ultimate test: a 100-foot ascent. Each stage was designed to build our confidence and skill, preparing us for the final, most difficult challenge. The thought was daunting, but I was resolute. As I prepared for the big day, I imagined myself drawing a deep breath and steeling myself, before plunging into the murky depths of the tower.

The key to surviving a submarine escape lies in breath control. As you ascend, the air in your lungs expands rapidly due to decreasing pressure. Without continuous exhalation, your lungs could explode. This terrifying possibility loomed over us, and we were forced to confront it head-on during our training. Each ascent was going to be a test of not just physical endurance but also mental discipline. We had to remain calm and focused, controlling our breathing despite the panic that threatened to set in.

Yet, amidst the rigours of escape training, I faced an unexpected obstacle, one far less scary than that tower of water, but which nonetheless nearly scuppered my naval career, before it had even started.

In a moment of youthful recklessness, I had left the base, taken the liberty boat (the vessel that transported sailors across the water to Portsmouth) and had a tattoo inked on my shoulder. It was, I thought, a magnificent depiction of an old British naval galleon at sea, with the sun setting on the horizon and 'Royal Navy' emblazoned beneath it. The tattoo was a testament to my love for the sea and my commitment to my path. Impressive though it was, that tattoo was also a massive mistake. The next day, my skin was still raw and tender from the tattoo artist's needle—in effect, a fresh wound that had not yet healed. And the day in question happened to be the day of my escape training!

That morning, we were lined up in our dressing gowns and as the instructor walked past us, he happened to tap me on my shoulder. I winced in pain and the instructor noticed, immediately asking me to remove my gown. I was a bit reluctant, as I knew what was coming.

'Take it off!' he barked, not expecting to have to ask a second time.

His eyes narrowed as he glimpsed my tattoo. 'When the fucking hell did you get that done?'

Stammering, I explained how I'd gone about it.

I could tell immediately that I was in big, big trouble. The instructor's face hardened as he listened to my explanation, his eyes filling with a mixture of anger and disappointment. Not only had I had an underage tattoo, but I had also taken the liberty boat without permission. Perhaps worse, I was now, due to the raw state of my skin, unable to participate in training.

The consequences were swift and went far beyond the confines of HMS Dolphin. In fact, rather bizarrely, the issue escalated up the chain of command, reaching the highest echelons of the Navy! Whispers of disciplinary action and a promising career cut short filled the air. Some even speculated that I had gotten the tattoo as a cry for help and that I was likely to take my own life! There was a stigma attached to such a brazen act of defiance, but also severe implications for the chain of command. How had I been allowed to escape?

Amidst all this turmoil, Warrant Officer Duckworth, who was responsible for all juniors on the base, emerged as an unlikely ally. He decided to shine an uncomfortable light on the Navy's failure to adequately supervise me—how it had allowed a young recruit to escape the base—and fought to retain me with a ferocity I will never forget. He was a seasoned veteran, a man who had seen it all and understood what really mattered. He saw beyond my mistakes, recognising my potential and determination. He was also a man who senior officers were willing to listen to.

Thanks to his intervention, I avoided the worst punishments. A month later, I found myself back at the water tower, ready to retake the escape training. The time away had given me a chance to reflect and prepare, both mentally and physically. I knew I could not afford another mistake.

This time, given how I'd screwed things up on the last occasion, there was no room for error. Focusing all my energy, I breathed out continuously, making a controlled ascent from the depths. It was gruelling, but I refused to give up. As I ascended, I could feel the pressure decreasing, the air in my lungs expanding. It was a constant battle to maintain control, to keep breathing out steadily. When I finally emerged from the water, gasping for air, I felt a profound sense of pride and accomplishment. I had pushed myself to my physical and mental limits and emerged stronger, more resilient, and more determined than ever.

With renewed purpose, I threw myself into my submarine training. The path ahead was challenging, with obstacles and setbacks at every turn, but I was ready to overcome them and earn my place among the best.

The real test loomed on the horizon: my first deployment —on board HMS Dreadnought. Aged just 16, I was about to be plunged headfirst into the shadowy undersea front of the Cold War, playing a pivotal role in tracking and gathering intelligence on Soviet submarines.

The Captains Guard being reviewed by the Captain before at Sunday Divisions.

HMS Raleigh Sunday Parade

Name of Ship (If Tender, insert also Parent Ship in brackets)	S. or N.S. (a)	Rate	Sub Branch	From (b)	To (c)	Cause of Discharge and other Notations authorised by Q.R. (R.N.)
RALEIGH	NS	JS(O)2.		30 AUG 77	27 NOV 77	
DOLPHIN	N	JSI(S)		28 NOV 77	20 AUG 78	
DOLPHIN	NS	JSI(S)(SM)		21 AUG 78	6 AUG 78	
NEPTUNE	NS	JSI(S)(SM)		7 AUG 78	9 AUG 78	
DREADNOUGHT (NEPTUNE)	S	JSI(S)(SM)		10 AUG 78	25 JAN 79	
DREADNOUGHT (PEMBROKE)	NS	JSI(S)(SM)		26 JAN 79	7 JAN 79	
CONQUEROR (NEPTUNE)	S	JSI(S)(SM)		8 JAN 79	10 FEB 79	
CONQUEROR (NEPTUNE)	NS	SIS(SM)		11 FEB 79	27 JAN 80	
CONQUEROR (NEPTUNE)	S	AAB(S)(SM)		28 JAN 80	10 FEB 80	
CONQUEROR (NEPTUNE)	S	AB(S)(SM)		11 FEB 80	14 SEP 80	
NEPTUNE	NS	AB(S)(SM)		15 SEP 80	5 JULY 81	
TRAFALGAR (NEPTUNE)	NS	AB(S)(SM)		6 JULY 81	1 OCT 82	
TRAFALGAR (NEPTUNE)	NS	ALB(S)(SM)		2 OCT 82	15 OCT 82	
TRAFALGAR (NEPTUNE)	S	ALS(S)(SM)		16 OCT 82	2 DEC 82	
DOLPHIN	NS	ALS(S)(SM)		3 DEC 82	7 MCH 83	
TURBULENT (NEPTUNE)	NS	ALS(S)(SM).		8 MCH 83	27 OCT 83	— 2 OCT 83.
TURBULENT (NEPTUNE)	S	ALS (S)	(SM)	28 OCT 83		
TURBULENT (NEPTUNE)	S	LS (S)	(SM)		31 OCT 84	
TURBULENT (DRAKE)	S	LS(S)	(SM)	1 NOV 84	8 JAN 85	PROMOTED

Name of Ship (If Tender, insert also Parent) Ship in brackets	S. or N.S. (a)

QUALIFICATIO

(To include attain

Date	Particulars
20 SEP 77	NAWET 2:2
3 MAR 79	Awarded Sm Badge
16 DEC 81	PVR for ALS (S)(SM)
4 MCH 83	PASSED PROF FOR LS(S) (SM)
10 SEP 84	COMPLETED LRLC

WOUNDS RECEIVED IN A

Date	
8 NOV 82	CW PAPERS RA

My service record

5. COLD WAR WARRIOR

I t was January 1978, and at the tender age of 16, I joined my first submarine posting on HMS Dreadnought in Hull, where the boat was docked for a few days. This was the beginning of an intense, often surreal journey that would shape my life in ways I couldn't have possibly imagined.

Dreadnought was the UK's first nuclear-powered submarine, built by Vickers-Armstrong in Barrow-in-Furness and commissioned into service in 1963—a hunter-killer boat designed to protect the deterrent and keep Britain safe. With a crew of roughly 150, she was a formidable vessel, half British and half American in design. At one point, a sign even marked the transition: 'You are now entering the American sector.' This hybrid nature of the submarine reflected the unique collaboration between the two nations, a partnership forged in the crucible of Cold War tensions.

People sometimes assume the Cold War refers to the nature of the conflict, that it was somehow lacking the 'heat' of an actual battle. But the truth is that it was called 'cold' because the majority of skirmishes took place in the freezing waters of the North Atlantic and below the ice of the Arctic. And as a submariner, I was in the thick of it.

At this point it might be worth setting the scene, as well as briefly explaining the role submarines played—and continue to play—beneath the ice.

In the 1960s, 1970s and 1980s, when the world's two superpowers jostled for dominance, a realm of secrecy and danger existed out of sight—submarine operations beneath the frozen surface. Here, beneath metres of ice, submarines became the silent sentinels, navigating treacherous waters to gather intelligence, maintain deterrence and, if necessary, strike against hostile forces.

During the Cold War, the Arctic was a battleground of strategic importance. Superpowers vied for control of polar territories, and beneath the ice, submarines played a crucial role in surveillance and

deterrence. Silent and elusive, they prowled the frigid waters, their mission to monitor enemy movements and, if required, unleash devastating firepower.

Submarines operating under the ice face a myriad of challenges. Thick layers of ice can impede communication and navigation while shifting ice floes pose a constant threat of detection. We submariners had to rely on cutting-edge sonar technology and our own expertise to navigate safely through the icy labyrinth, evading detection by enemy forces.

The key to submarine operations under the ice, then as now, is stealth. Submarines must operate with near-total silence, minimising acoustic signatures to avoid detection by hostile forces. Advanced propulsion systems and sound-dampening technologies enable submarines to glide silently through the water, virtually invisible to enemy sensors.

Submarines serve as the eyes and ears of their respective navies, collecting vital intelligence on enemy movements and capabilities. Equipped with state-of-the-art surveillance systems, submarines could covertly monitor enemy activities, providing invaluable information to military commanders.

The mere presence of submarines beneath the ice served as a powerful deterrent against aggression in the Cold War. The knowledge that unseen adversaries lurked beneath the frozen surface compelled the Soviets to tread cautiously, lest they provoke a devastating response from lurking submarines.

Submarine operations under the ice represent the pinnacle of naval warfare, combining stealth, precision and strategic foresight. In the frozen depths of the Arctic, submarines stood ready to defend national interests, deter aggression and uphold the balance of power in an ever-dangerous world.

When the time comes to act, submarines are capable of executing precision strikes against enemy targets with unparalleled accuracy. Whether launching cruise missiles from submerged positions or conducting covert insertions of special operations forces, submarines possess the versatility to project power and influence deep into enemy territory.

One of the key advantages of submarine operations is their inherent deniability. Unlike overt military actions that risk escalation, submarine operations can be conducted covertly, allowing governments to deny involvement if necessary. This ambiguity adds an extra layer of complexity to the strategic calculus of rival powers in the region—today, and during the Cold War.

The sad truth is that the Arctic remains a potential flashpoint for conflict. Tensions between rival powers have escalated in recent years, raising concerns about the possibility of a confrontation beneath the ice. In such a scenario, submarines will be playing a central role, poised to execute precise strikes against enemy targets.

*

Before I came to truly understand the Cold War role I was playing, there was life as a submariner to become accustomed to. There was no naval base in Hull, so to begin with, we submariners lived in hotels, only allowed out at night in our uniforms so the Military Police officers, who patrolled the streets ensuring we didn't get up to excessive mischief, could keep an eye on us. Those uniforms made us targets for aggression from the locals, who resented our presence, mainly because they also made us popular with the young women. You have to understand that at the time, women in places like Hull, where men had limited prospects, saw submariners as a 'meal ticket' to a better life, with the promise of married quarters and a pension.

I remember one brief romance with a local girl in Hull. We ended up in my hotel room, which I shared with a chap called Tiny, who was ironically named as he was in fact 6'3"! As the girl and I went at it like a couple of rabbits, Tiny lay there grinning like a Cheshire cat. Bless him. I remember this poor girl glimpsing him at one point and being very affronted, but to be fair there wasn't much room for privacy!

It wasn't the most gallant act, but after our encounter, I gave the girl a made-up telephone number. I was not ready for marriage!

Living in a crowded room in a hotel in Hull was one thing. Life on board was something else. It was unlike anything I had ever experienced. The was even less privacy of course, but there were also confined spaces and limited washing facilities. It took some getting used to.

I remember boarding HMS Dreadnought for the very first time. What hit me initially was the smell—a pungent whiff of body odour, inescapable in such close quarters. It was an ever-present reminder of the sacrifices and challenges of submarine life.

As I soon discovered, the camaraderie among submariners is unique. The close quarters and shared experiences create bonds that are unbreakable. We relied on each other not just for professional support but for personal strength as well. In the depths of the ocean, far from home and family, our crewmates become our closest confidants and allies.

One of the most challenging aspects of submarine life was isolation. For weeks or even months at a time, we were cut off from the outside world, relying on sporadic communications to stay in touch with our loved ones. The lack of natural light, the constant hum of the engine and the electrics, and the confined space could take a toll on even the strongest minds. But we learned to adapt, finding ways to maintain our morale and mental health.

There were games and activities, which I'll touch on later, but there were also strict rules and regulations, to ensure we all knew what lines couldn't be crossed. The consequences for breaking those rules were severe. Thieves, in particular, were treated very brutally. I heard stories of them having their hands crushed in hydraulic doors as punishment. The submarine's confined environment meant that trust and reliability were paramount; any breach was dealt with harshly to maintain discipline and order.

My role on board was as a sonar operator, listening for Soviet submarines and warships. Each vessel had a distinct sound, determined by the propellers and the propulsion chain (the shaft and the engine, in other words). It was a skill that required intense concentration and a keen ear. The constant hum of the ocean and the subtle differences in sound became my second language. It was both an art and a science, a delicate balance of intuition and technical knowledge.

We operated in certain areas and 'layers' of the ocean, determined by the varying temperatures and densities of the water. These layers acted like underwater walls for sound, with certain frequencies propagating differently depending on the conditions. Typically, the ocean was divided into three sections: the shallow thermocline (0-200 feet), the middle thermocline (200-800 feet), and the deep thermocline (800 feet and beyond). However, these values could vary greatly depending on the ocean, weather conditions and temperature.

My first taste of life at sea came as we headed straight out into the North Sea. We hit a horrible patch where the North Sea meets the Irish Sea, and I experienced terrible seasickness in a Force 8 gale. We couldn't dive because there was something beneath us—in all likelihood a Soviet sub—a reminder of the constant danger we faced. This was a baptism by fire, a harsh introduction to the unpredictable nature of submarine operations.

Underwater, sonar became both our eyes and ears. We had to stay silent, listening for any hint of enemy activity. Sometimes, in the quieter moments, we would hear whale songs carried for miles through the depths. It was an enchanting sound, completely distracting from the tension of our mission. The beauty of the whale song was a stark contrast to the grim reality of our work, a fleeting moment of serenity in an otherwise high-stress environment.

As we dived deeper, the pressure would build, compressing the submarine. Some panels would even bend under the immense force. I remember one navigator who wore pyjamas on board—a strange quirk that was somehow tolerated by the captain. On one occasion, someone put his pyjamas inside a panel that had opened up, which then snapped shut as we rose and the pressure outside decreased, trapping them inside. He went mad when he couldn't wear his beloved pyjamas! These small incidents provided a much-needed break from the monotony and tension of life underwater.

After my stint on Dreadnought, I joined HMS Conqueror in January 1979. At 17, I was the youngest on board. We were based in Faslane, Scotland, and I remember a bungalow opposite the base that everyone knew was home to Russian spies, keeping tabs on our comings and goings. This constant surveillance added another layer of tension to our already stressful lives.

Life on a submarine could be intense, with long periods at sea and little contact with the outside world. When we returned to base, we would be locked in a bar in Faslane to decompress for 24 hours. The idea was that we would get drunk and then take out all our pent-up aggression on each other, rather than bringing it home to our wives and children which, sadly, had been known to happen. We'd then emerge from the bar a day later, bruised and battered, all that angst and tension finally released before we went home to our families. This ritual, which might seem brutal and a touch barbaric to an outsider, was in fact crucial for maintaining our mental health and camaraderie and conserving marriages and family life, which was already under threat from the long stints at sea that we submariners underwent.

I'll never forget the feeling when the submarine hatch first opened after a long patrol. The air below was so filtered, so consistent and pure, that the first hit of 'fresh' air above, filled with particulates of fuel and other substances, would make me feel sick to my stomach. It was a strange paradox—the air that should have felt refreshing instead made me nauseous. It was a stark reminder of the alien world we lived in beneath the waves.

On HMS Conqueror, I joined a tight-knit crew, many of whom had spent decades on the same boat. As the new kid, I had to earn my place. Our primary mission was to protect the nuclear deterrent, but as the Cold War intensified, the Russians began targeting us directly. We became the predators, hunting Soviet subs. This shift in roles from the hunted to the hunter brought its own set of challenges and dangers.

I spent countless hours tracking and gathering intelligence on Soviet submarines. It was tense, often tedious work, but the adrenaline rush of going up against the enemy made it all worthwhile. Over the course of my time on Conqueror, three Soviet subs were 'sunk' on my sonar bearings deep under the Arctic ice. Looking back now, it's a sobering thought that men died as a result of my actions. But we were at war, and if it hadn't been them, it might have been the nation's deterrent, or indeed us.

After each successful mission, we would celebrate with special 'Sods' Operas'—raucous affairs featuring skits, songs and submariners in drag that were totally unique to the submarine service. Submariners took the performances very seriously. Some crew members even packed dresses before they boarded so they had the right costume for their part! As the youngest on board, I was often roped into playing a puppet with someone's hand up the back of my shirt, making me dance or lip-sync. Once, after a war games exercise in the Mediterranean, which I'll describe in more detail in Chapter 7, we made so much noise that the Americans actually got in touch to say they'd 'sunk' us. Our captain replied that we had, in fact, already sunk them! These moments of levity were essential for maintaining our sanity and morale.

But life on a submarine wasn't all action and excitement. Much of our time was spent on long, boring patrols, with little to do except maintain equipment and stay vigilant. The food was basic, and the living conditions were cramped. There was no privacy to speak of, and we had to be ready to act at a moment's notice. The monotony was punctuated by brief bursts of activity, creating a rhythm that was both exhausting and strangely comforting.

I remember one particular break in Brixham in February. Our captain, in his wisdom, decided that we should go ashore and get pissed to let off some steam before heading home. We anchored off the coast and took a boat in early in the evening. It was a night of heavy drinking in the pubs, and at one point, the captain even took us to a nightclub. But by the time we staggered outside the club, we realised that he had disappeared, having already gone back to the boat. Worse still, when we made our way to the jetty, we discovered that there was no boat to take us back. We were stranded!

I remember our sonar officer, Charlie H, who was a real party animal, deciding that he'd bed down where he stood. 'I'm pissed, I'm tired,' he declared. 'I'm going to sleep.'

He then proceeded to wrap himself in fishing nets and pass out on the ground. The rest of us, half a dozen or so, ended up sleeping in a public toilet, where we wrapped ourselves in toilet roll for a little warmth. It was very basic, and I doubt I got even an hour of sleep.

The next morning, a police officer arrived as I was checking on Charlie. He kicked me, and I called him a twat in response. Charlie, God bless him, simply looked up and told the officer to fuck off. We all got arrested, of course, but at least we got to warm up in the cells for a bit!

Looking back, it's hard to believe that this bunch of pissheads were entrusted with the immense responsibility of protecting the nation's nuclear deterrent at such a young age. But the submarine service had a way of forging boys into men, of instilling a sense of duty and camaraderie that bound us together. The experiences we shared, both good and bad, created bonds that would last a lifetime. And crucially, no one works off a hangover quicker than a submariner, so there was never the feeling that we were drunk at the controls.

Those long patrols, the endless hours of boredom punctuated by moments of sheer terror, shaped us in ways that are hard to describe. We lived in a world within a world, a silent service operating in the shadows, unseen and unheard. The isolation and confinement tested our limits, both physically and mentally.

The Hunted and the Hunter

A British Nuclear Submarine returning from a long patrol. Having done this I knew how all the men onboard felt.

6. DIVING INTO DANGER

As a submariner, I thought I had faced every challenge the silent service could throw at me. But there was one frontier I had yet to conquer—the world outside the submarine's steel hull. It was a realm fraught with danger, where a single mistake could spell disaster for the entire crew. It was into this world that I volunteered to plunge when I signed up for Ships Diver training while still serving on HMS Conqueror.

Divers played a crucial role in the operation of a submarine. We were the eyes and hands of the vessel, responsible for inspecting the hull for damage or sabotage, clearing inlets and outlets, and carrying out repairs in hostile waters. One of our most critical tasks was checking for and removing limpet mines—small, magnetic explosives that could be attached to the hull by enemy divers. A single missed mine could sink a submarine, and it was our job to ensure that never happened.

Training to become a submarine diver was an arduous process designed to weed out all but the toughest and most determined. It took place at Hornsea Lake in Portsmouth, a man-made body of water half a mile long that had once been a torpedo firing range. From the moment we arrived, we were pushed to our limits, both physically and mentally.

Before the sun had risen, we were jolted awake for a pre-dawn run. The instructors had a knack for finding the steepest, most gruelling trails, pushing us to our physical limits. It wasn't just about building muscle, stamina and endurance, but about forging mental toughness and teaching us to push through pain and fatigue.

We would run for miles, our legs burning, lungs gasping in the damp, cold air. The camaraderie developed during these runs was incredible. We were all suffering together, encouraging one another to keep going and not give up. Swimming drills in the frigid waters of Hornsea Lake followed the runs. The shock of the cold water was brutal, but it was a necessary part of our conditioning.

One particular exercise I remember vividly involved dragging old tyres through the water. We were paired up, and our task was to take turns pulling our partner, who would lie on the tyre across the lake. This exercise simulated the effort required to rescue a fellow diver in distress. It was exhausting but taught us the importance of teamwork and the physical strength needed for such rescues.

One of the most challenging exercises was the half-mile underwater swim, where we had to make our way from one end of the lake to the other using just a single tank of air. It was a test of not just our swimming ability but also our ability to control our breathing, conserve our air supply, and stay calm under pressure.

As we progressed through the training, we learned many new skills. We practised diving in challenging conditions—at night, in strong currents, and in low visibility—to simulate the real-world scenarios we might face. We learned how to manage nitrogen narcosis, the disorienting effect that can occur at depth, and how to avoid decompression sickness (also known as 'the bends'), the potentially lethal condition caused by ascending too quickly.

Divers played a crucial role in the operation of a submarine, acting as the eyes and hands of the vessel. They were responsible for inspecting the hull for damage or sabotage, clearing inlets and outlets, and carrying out repairs in hostile waters. One of the most critical tasks was checking for and removing limpet mines—small, magnetic explosives that enemy divers could attach to the hull. Missing a single mine could sink a submarine, so the divers' training included learning how to handle these mines. This required a delicate touch and nerves of steel, as the mines were designed to be challenging to detect and disarm. Practising with dummy mines, divers honed their skills until they could perform the task almost by instinct, ensuring the safety of the submarine.

The most memorable part of my training was the final exercise: a simulated hull inspection on an actual submarine. We were divided into teams and assigned different sections of the hull to inspect. Our task was to identify potential threats or damage and report our findings. This exercise was as close to a real-world scenario as possible and was both exhilarating and nerve-wracking.

My team was responsible for the stern section near the propeller shaft. Our torches cut through the murky water as we moved along the hull, illuminating the cold, grey steel. Every few minutes, we would stop to inspect a particular area more closely, looking for anything out of the ordinary. Knowing that a single mistake could jeopardise the entire crew kept us focused and alert.

The sense of accomplishment was overwhelming when we finally surfaced and reported our findings. We had completed the most challenging part of our training and were now qualified submarine divers. Our bond was stronger than ever, forged through shared hardship and the knowledge that we could rely on each other in the most dangerous situations.

After qualifying as a ship diver, I served in that capacity on several different boats. It was a demanding role, often requiring us to dive at a moment's notice, even if we were exhausted from long watches or other duties. We had to constantly check and maintain our equipment, ensuring every piece was in perfect working order. A faulty valve or a torn seam in a dry suit could be fatal at depth.

But for all the challenges and dangers, diving was also an incredibly thrilling experience. There was something almost meditative about the silence and weightlessness, the feeling of being suspended in an alien world. Of course, there were moments of terror, too—tangles in the guide ropes, equipment failures, close encounters with some very large fish, sharks or other dangerous sea life.

My first deployment as a qualified diver was back on HMS Conqueror. One of our most critical tasks was to inspect the hull for any signs of damage or sabotage. This required us to dive beneath the submarine, sometimes in treacherous conditions, to check every inch of the hull. The waters of the North Atlantic were often cold and pitch black, adding to the task's difficulty. But we had been trained to handle these conditions and took pride in our ability to perform our duties under the most challenging circumstances.

About to start a huge NATO exercise lasting 6 weeks in the North Atlantic

7. SUBMARINE SECRETS AND SURPRISES

Life aboard HMS Conqueror was a series of intense, challenging and often surprising experiences. As I adapted to my role as a sonar operator, I quickly realised that the underwater world we navigated was filled with complexities and dangers that demanded the highest levels of skill and ingenuity. But there was also fun to be had in some scheduled and unscheduled moments of downtime.

One of the most memorable episodes during my early days on Conqueror occurred during a run ashore in Gibraltar. What was supposed to be a brief week-long port call turned into an extended stay of eight weeks due to issues with the reactor compartment. This unexpected delay led to a unique and somewhat surreal experience for the crew. Half of us were billeted in hotels on the leeward side of the Rock, while the other half were crammed into army barracks on the windward side.

The two groups were separated by a tunnel running through the Rock, an impressive feat of engineering that also served as an underground storehouse for the British outpost's supplies and ammunition. Navigating this labyrinthine tunnel system, with its echoing chambers and dimly lit passageways, was fascinating.

The barracks, in contrast, were far from fascinating. Packed tightly with soldiers, whom we affectionately called 'Pongos' ('wherever the Army goes, the pong goes,' as the saying went!), we often found ourselves in minor conflicts fuelled by cheap alcohol and inter-service rivalry. Fights became a nightly occurrence, with battered and bruised soldiers stumbling back to their bunks in the early hours.

Every now and then, we swapped over, and I found myself enjoying a much more pleasant experience in a luxury hotel. I have fond memories of lounging by the rooftop pool, savouring the Mediterranean sun, and appreciating the rare moments of tranquillity away from the confined quarters of the submarine. Gibraltar itself was a treasure trove of history and culture. I explored its winding streets, discovering lively pubs, historic churches and charming chapels at every turn.

However, Gibraltar presented a dichotomy that was a bit troubling. During the day, the beaches were filled with beautiful women basking in the sun. Yet, as evening approached, they vanished, reflecting the conservative culture prevalent in Spain at the time. This stark contrast was a subtle reminder to us submariners to respect local customs and boundaries. Put another way, the local ladies were strictly out of bounds!

Our time in Gibraltar eventually came to an end, and we sailed into the Mediterranean, prepared to face the challenges ahead. The Mediterranean operations were intense, often involving war games with the American Fifth Fleet. These exercises tested our skills to the limit. One particularly memorable exercise had us trailing two American submarines, utilising their acoustic blind spots to remain undetected. We gathered intelligence on their movements and tactics for hours, a thrilling cat-and-mouse game beneath the waves.

When the Americans finally sensed our presence, their shock was palpable. The sight of a small British submarine outmanoeuvring the pride of the US Navy was a moment of triumph for us and of humiliation for the Yanks. It showcased our technical prowess and the cunning and resourcefulness that defined HMS Conqueror.

Not all port calls were as pleasant as Gibraltar, however. A stop in Naples left a distinctly bad taste in the mouth. On arrival, we found the harbour filled with oily water and debris. As a newly minted diver, I was relieved not to have to plunge into that foul mix. Despite these conditions, Naples had its charms, including grand churches and ornately decorated chapels, as well as the haunting ruins of Pompeii. Walking through the ancient city, frozen in time by volcanic ash, was a sobering reminder of nature's power and the excruciating death that had befallen the residents centuries before.

One of the more unsettling experiences in Naples involved a suspicious man who appeared to be following me and my shipmates from bar to bar. My suspicions grew when he finally approached me, striking up a conversation in flawless English. Claiming to be an Englishman working for an electronics firm linked to BAE Systems, he began probing me for details about Conqueror's equipment and capabilities. His story didn't add up, and I soon realised he was likely a foreign agent.

I played along, feeding him a mixture of truths and fabrications while trying to extract more information about his true identity. When I returned to Conqueror, I reported the encounter to my superiors. Weeks later, I was called into the captain's cabin, where I assumed I was about to be given a bollocking. Imagine my surprise when I was informed I'd been given a commendation from the First Sea Lord no less for helping catch a spy. Sadly, as the work of the security services was covert, I never received a written letter. But hearing the captain reading out the contents of a signal he had received about my actions, which was then destroyed, was still a moment of pride—and a reminder of the constant need for secrecy and discretion in the submarine service

I was away on Conqueror for about six months; by the time I returned, I was an acting leading hand. Rising through the ranks was to come easy to me, but not without some serious training and study, as I was to discover.

HMS Trafalgar on the move I was on the bridge as the lookout.

8. RISING THROUGH THE RANKS

After proving myself on Conqueror, new opportunities and responsibilities came my way. My old friend Andy encouraged me to apply for a Trafalgar-class sub at Barrow. It was a good decision, one that would lead to advanced training courses, earned promotions and faced the challenges of leadership. Along the way, I gained a deeper appreciation for the technical and human elements that make an effective submarine crew.

While waiting for my transfer to Trafalgar to come through, I was assigned to guard duty at the Polaris Building in Faslane. It was a monotonous job, checking passes by day and patrolling endless corridors by night. But I knew it was just a temporary stop on my journey, and I was eager to see what challenges lay ahead.

In July 1981, I finally made my way to Barrow, where HMS Trafalgar was still being built. It was an exciting time, as the crew was being assembled and trained while the submarine took shape in the shipyard. Because there was no armed forces base with accommodation in Barrow, we were paid a daily allowance and allowed to live where we wanted, much as we had done in Hull before. It was a level of freedom I hadn't experienced in a while, with no real naval restrictions and the ability to go out on the town, albeit in uniform, enjoying the same 'benefits' I had in Hull.

I ended up living in a lovely bed and breakfast, while by day I worked alongside civilians—joiners, electricians and other tradesmen—as we prepared Trafalgar for her maiden voyage. It was a massive undertaking, and the sheer scale of the operation struck me. To even launch the submarines, thousands of tons of sand had to be removed from the seabed, a feat that sounded mad but was made possible by the skill and dedication of the Barrow workforce.

When the time finally came for Trafalgar to set out, we had to wait for the February spring tide. Our first order of business was a deep dive to test the submarine's watertight integrity. The port pilot who had guided us out was none too pleased when rough seas forced him to stay on board for the entirety of the week-long dive and testing period. We had engineers from the shipyard with us, checking and double-checking every system to ensure we were ready for active service.

We returned to Barrow for the commissioning ceremony after passing our initial tests with flying colours. In this grand affair, a dignitary smashed a bottle of champagne against Trafalgar's hull, officially welcoming her into the fleet. From there, it was straight into action, as we joined a massive NATO exercise alongside Danish frigates, American destroyers and British warships. We took turns playing the 'enemy' role, testing our allies' ability to detect and engage us.

One particularly memorable scenario had us playing 'dead,' cutting our engines and letting the submarine drift slowly down until we sat silently on the seabed, some 650 feet below the surface. Waiting in the darkness was an eerie experience, wondering if our opponents would sniff us out.

But the real surprise came when the Americans introduced an unannounced player—a submarine tasked with taking on the role of a Soviet vessel. It caught everyone off guard, but our captain was quick to react. He positioned us between the 'Soviet' sub and the exercise fleet, then ordered us to make as much noise as possible. We blasted music, banged on the hull, and even turned on all the televisions. The racket made it impossible for the other sub to listen in on the exercise, and as soon as it moved, we slipped in behind it, shadowing it for a full day while collecting valuable data. The following day, we 'sank' it with a simulated torpedo shot, a testament to our skill and cunning.

As we continued participating in exercises and deployments, I had the opportunity to share a bit of my world with my father, possibly in a last-ditch attempt to win his approval. On Father's Day, I invited him and his best friend, Ernie, to Faslane for a visit. It was a somewhat strained relationship—many of the crew seemed to assume Ernie was my dad, given how much we looked alike and how he treated me compared to my father's constant criticism. I noticed the resemblance too, and wondered briefly whether this was the real source of my father's lifelong irritation with me, but I tried not to dwell on it. That part of my life was well behind me.

The visit did give my father a glimpse into the realities of submarine life. He couldn't believe we were going to sea with the same submariners he'd seen getting blinding drunk in the pub the night before. But the following day, as we set off and dived to 200 feet, he saw those same men, sober and professional, handling their duties with skill and focus. 'That guy was completely off his trolley last night,' he told me in the control room. 'Now he's the most professional man I've ever seen.' It was a small victory, getting that grudging respect, even if Ernie's presence—and all the comments it prompted —dampened the day somewhat.

As I progressed in my career, I attended specialised training in sonar operation, submarine systems, and escape and rescue procedures. I also spent time at the Naval Weapons School, becoming familiar with the torpedoes and other armaments.

One of the most formative experiences of career progression was a leadership course in Scotland, where a bunch of potential leading rates drawn from across the Navy were split into teams of four and had to navigate the Ochil Hills, all while carrying heavy packs weighing around 40 kg containing a map, compass, knife, rations, water and cooking kit, and completing tasks along the way. It was already a tough environment, which was then made worse by members of the Parachute Regiment (Paras), who'd regularly goad and distract us, to make life even harder.

As the only submariner on the course, I was aware I was representing the service. Naval ships offer plenty of opportunities to keep fit on deck, while the confined spaces of a submarine make that much harder. So I'd trained hard before Scotland to make sure I kept up with the others and didn't let the service down!

The nights were a particular challenge. On one, we slept huddled together under an overhang, only to be jolted awake by the Paras tossing flash-bangs at us just before dawn, an exercise that was meant to disorientate and confuse us, when we'd already had very little sleep. Then it was up and running, a mile or more through the predawn darkness before the day's main march began.

I'll never forget the evening we descended into a pair of fields, one pristine, the other filled with cows and dotted with steaming pats of shit.

A Scots lad from the group that had arrived just before us stood up and lobbed a chunk of dung in our direction, shouting, 'Hello, lads—welcome to Shite City!' It was a moment of hilarity in an otherwise gruelling experience.

On the very last day, the rules changed. No longer was it just about getting from start to finish—now we had to collect objects along the way. The stakes were high. The winning team would be transported back to the barracks. The second would endure a short walk to the nearest village, before being picked up. The team in third place faced a longer trek, and the fourth an even more daunting hike. In the end, our team came out on top, a testament to the bonds we had forged through shared hardship. I was delighted!

The leadership training, emphasising teamwork, communication and problem-solving, served me well as I continued to rise through the ranks. By the age of 22, I had been promoted to Leading Hand. And just three months into my posting on HMS Turbulent, my superiors encouraged me to consider officer training.

The two main routes to becoming an officer were joining straight out of school or working your way up through the ranks. There were two paths for those of us coming up from the lower decks. The faster one, the one I was on, was known as 'Upper Yardsman.' The other, Special Duties, was a slower learning process on the job, rarely leading to command posts.

Being an Upper Yardsman wasn't easy. At a stroke, you were neither a rating nor an officer, and as such, you became a slight pariah. The only way to overcome other people's antagonism or suspicion was to earn respect, which I did.

I pursued a commission and began instruction at the Royal Naval College in Dartmouth in 1985. I was very aware I was entering an illustrious institution filled with cadets from a very different social standing to me—the sons of Lords, Dukes and Earls among them. Despite the challenges, I was determined to show that I could compete well with my privileged classmates. The intense training involved physical and mental strain, but I was committed to succeeding. I remember a moment when I supported a struggling classmate—a man hoping to become a naval medical officer, who was not in peak fitness. He was already a commander, while I was a humble midshipman. It was during a demanding run up the killer hill from the quay to the college when I saw him in difficulty. I was determined to help, as failure meant the end of his dreams.

'Come on,' I said. 'You and me are going to get up this hill.'

Step by step, we pushed on, until he finally stumbled across the finish line and collapsed into my arms. 'Thank you,' he gasped. 'You've saved my naval career.' I just smiled and clapped him on the shoulder. 'We're all cut from the same cloth, sir. Some of us just have a finer weave than others.'

That moment typified my approach to officer training. I knew I didn't have the same background as many of my peers. I hadn't gone to the 'right' schools and didn't have the 'right' accent or connections. But I had grit, determination and a rock-solid belief in the value of teamwork and mutual support.

As I progressed through the three stages of training—the classroom-based juniors phase, a stint at sea for fleet time and the more hands-on seniors phase—I continued to face challenges and obstacles.

During my fleet time, I had the privilege of serving on HMS Swift in Malaysia and Hong Kong, where I had a fabulous time being treated to a private box, a la carte dinner and a private betting stall at Happy Valley Races.

I also witnessed the remarkable work of the Gurkhas and their guard dogs on the border with China. I remember there were two parallel fences at the border, and the most enormous Alsatians patrolling in between. One of the Gurkhas decided to introduce me to the dog he was handling. Now I'd faced a lot of scary challenges in my time, but I was absolutely crapping myself as the dog approached me! I remember the man telling me to put out my hand. This seemed like a really bad idea, but I did what I was told. To my delight, the dog licked it, and then my face. After this, the huge animal placed his paw on my shoulder. Was this positive? I didn't know!

'The dog has now bonded with you,' said the Gurkha. 'It will never leave your side.'

He was right about that. That night, I had to sleep with the bleeding thing!

That time on the border was fascinating. After the glitz and glamour of the races, it was a humbling experience to see the poverty and hardship in that region.

The final stint of my fleet time was on board HMS Gloucester, a Type 42 destroyer. It was, I have to say, a mundane deployment in the Atlantic with the US, tracking Soviet subs, an exercise I was far happier taking part in underwater!

Back at Dartmouth for the senior phase, I grappled with the entrenched class system permeating every aspect of college life. Some of my classmates, especially those from public school backgrounds, seemed to revel in the hierarchy, lording their status over those of us from more humble origins. I did my best to avoid them, focusing instead on building bonds with those who shared my values.

One such friendship was with Abdul Aziz, a fellow cadet from Dubai. He and I became close, watching each other's backs as we navigated the training challenges. It wasn't until the end of our time together that he revealed his father was a prince—a fact that, to our credit, didn't change a thing about our relationship. When the course ended, he told me that I had an open invitation to visit him in Dubai. All I had to do was let him know when I was arriving, and he'd send a limo to fetch me from the airport. Years later, the invitation to visit him in his homeland still stands, which says so much about the enduring nature of our forged connections. I've never taken it up though. Perhaps I prefer to remember me and Abdul as two officer cadets, as opposed to me and a prince!

As the final exams loomed, the pressure mounted. Eleven gruelling tests stood between us and our commissions. To my disgust, I learned that some of my more privileged peers had found a way to cheat the system, positioning the student who'd become an expert in each subject at the centre of the exam room, where their papers could be easily copied. This system was then adapted for the next exam when the new 'expert' took the central seat. It was a blatant abuse of their advantages, and it left me seething.

Even more annoying was the knowledge that a well-placed 'bung'—a bribe or donation—could sometimes be the difference between passing and failing. I knew of one of my classmates, the son of a wealthy family, who had his percentage mark adjusted from 54 to 55, enabling him to scrape by. Another cadet, who had scored a 54 on his own merits, was failed and dismissed. The injustice of it all left a bitter taste in my mouth.

But I refused to let a handful of bad apples' actions tarnish my achievements. When I graduated from Dartmouth as a newly minted sub-lieutenant, I did so with my head held high, knowing I had earned my place through hard work and dedication.

From there, it was on to HMS Trenchant and a deployment that would test my skills and resolve like never before. But before I could embark on that next chapter, I had one last adventure to undertake.

For three months, I found myself assigned to HMS Fife, a frigate with the distinction of being the first British warship to sail through the St Lawrence Seaway and into the Great Lakes of the US for 20 years or more. It was a journey that took us to cities like Milwaukee, Chicago and St Johns, a whirlwind tour of North America that opened my eyes to the vastness and diversity of the world beyond the confines of the submarine service.

One particular moment stands out in my memory. As we were transiting the seaway, the captain got it into his head that he wanted to navigate a particularly treacherous stretch of water, one filled with icebergs carved from the nearby glaciers. Despite the protestations of his officers, who pointed out the dangers of taking a warship into such an obstacle course, he insisted on forging ahead.

And so we found ourselves picking our way through a field of frozen behemoths, some as large as the ship itself. At one point, a helicopter was dispatched to drop me onto the surface of one of the larger bergs, a surreal experience that drove home the incredible power and beauty of the natural world.

Surrounded by an endless expanse of white, I felt humility and perspective wash over me. It was a reminder that no matter my accomplishments, there would always be something larger than myself to strive for. With that sense of purpose, I stepped forward into the next phase of my career, ready to face whatever trials and triumphs the future might hold.

Dressed to impress, on the day of my passing out parade - December 1985.

BRNC, the place that changed my life.

BRNC from a different angle.

9. DEEP TROUBLE

L ife on board a submarine was never without risk, but some patrols pushed us to our limits. As I took on new roles and responsibilities, I found myself facing challenges that tested not only my professional skills but also my personal resilience and ability to endure unrelenting pressure.

In 1988, I served as the ship's communication officer at HMS Trenchant. Much of our operational time was spent in the Baltic or under the ice, in an environment that was as alien as it was unforgiving. The sound of silence was all-encompassing, broken only by the occasional hull creak or equipment hum. There was little in the way of marine life—a few fish, perhaps, but mostly an endless expanse of plankton drifting like ghostly clouds through the dark water.

We relied on two cameras mounted on the submarine's exterior to navigate this eerie landscape. One was forward-facing, designed to pick up any obstacles or hazards in our path. More than once, we were startled by the sudden appearance of large, menacing shapes looming out of the gloom, only to realise, upon closer inspection, that they were nothing more than dense clusters of plankton, magnified by the camera lens.

The other camera was trained upwards, scanning the underside of the ice pack for any breaks or openings. This was a critical task, as in the event of an engine failure, we would have only three hours of diesel power to find a way to the surface. The diesel engines required oxygen to run, and a means to expel exhaust, and the only place to find either was at the surface, in the open air.

During this particular deployment, we were operating alongside two American 688 class submarines. Our mission was to locate a new Soviet sub that was rumoured to have advanced capabilities that posed a significant threat to our forces. The Soviets had developed a hover mode that allowed their submarines to sit perfectly still beneath the ice. They ran their engines at a slow crawl to maintain position before launching their missiles.

Our job was to find these subs and then park ourselves behind them, monitoring their every move. The challenge was that they were rarely alone—an escort vessel was almost always nearby, watching and listening for any sign of enemy activity. If we were ever unlucky enough to hear the sound of missile hatches opening, we knew we would have only moments to act.

The protocol was to notify the command centre at Northwood immediately and await further instructions. We would all likely be given the order to destroy the asset—to launch our attack and eliminate the threat before it could strike. But we also knew that such an action would probably mean sacrificing ourselves. There would be little chance of escape or survival in the chaos and devastation that followed.

We had to learn to compartmentalise our thoughts and emotions to cope with these high-stakes missions' constant stress and pressure. We entered 'sea mode,' a state of hyper-focus and heightened alertness, allowing us to concentrate on the tasks.

A typical day would see us working six-hour shifts, grabbing meals (or 'scran,' as we called it) in between, and then spending any downtime catching up on paperwork or holding a precious hour or two of sleep. The Navy ran on paperwork, and even in the ocean's depths, there was always a stack of forms and reports that needed completing.

In truth, we were running on pure adrenaline most of the time. The constant vigilance and the knowledge that a single mistake could spell disaster for the entire crew was a weight that never fully lifted, even in moments of relative calm.

But there were lighter moments, too. I remember one occasion when a whale took a romantic interest in our submarine, sidling alongside us and making strange noises. We joked that it was trying to mate with us, this bizarre metal creature that had invaded its domain. Fortunately, the whale thought better of getting too close—perhaps deterred by the whirring of our propellers—and eventually swam off in search of a more suitable partner.

Another highlight of life on board was the weekly movie nights when 40 or 50 of us crammed into the mess to watch a film. For a couple of precious hours, we could allow ourselves to switch off, to forget about the dangers and responsibilities that awaited us outside that small, darkened room. The tradition of the 'Sods' Operas' continued. It still makes me laugh thinking of the men who brought dresses to sea with them so they could do some drag and entertain their crewmates.

As for alcohol, it was strictly rationed. The junior rates were allotted a small beer allowance, but most of us chose not to drink it. The risks were too high—when you're living and working in such close quarters, with lives depending on your every action, even a slight buzz could have disastrous consequences. Most crews went completely dry during patrols.

The crew's transformation was palpable when we finally surfaced after a long stint under the ice. We were closer and more bonded as a unit. We had been through something profound together, something those who had never experienced it could never fully understand. It was a camaraderie forged in shared adversity, and it would stay with us long after we returned to land.

After my time on Trenchant, I was selected to attend the Submarine Officers Advanced Warfare Course. This course is not a given. You are selected based on the reports your senior officers give you; you have to be good enough, in other words. The course is the final step before you go back to sea and are tried and tested, gain more experience in the command and control side of warfare onboard a Royal Navy Submarine. It was a chance to deepen my knowledge and skills and take on greater responsibilities within the service. But I quickly realised that there was one area where I was lacking—the use of the periscope to calculate the range and bearing of enemy warships.

It was a highly technical skill that required a keen eye and a deep understanding of the complex interplay of variables like wind speed, wave height, and the curvature of the Earth. While I excelled in most other aspects of the course—finishing top of my class in several subjects—I simply didn't have enough experience with the periscope to feel confident in my abilities.

I knew then that I wasn't ready for the Perisher course— the gruelling, make-or-break training programme that would qualify me to command my submarine. It was a harsh realisation but also a necessary one. I had to be honest about my strengths and weaknesses and focus on honing my skills where they were most needed.

In 1989, I was assigned to HMS Repulse, a Resolution-class ballistic missile submarine. It was an ageing boat with outdated technology and frequent mechanical problems that kept the engineering crew on their toes. But it was also a vital part of our nation's nuclear deterrent, tasked with carrying out long, silent patrols deep beneath the surface.

As the communications officer, I was responsible for all external and internal messaging—a role requiring the highest security clearance levels. Before joining Repulse, I spent a couple of weeks at GCHQ in Cheltenham, undergoing tests and interviews that elevated my clearance from top secret to 'top secret UK/US eyes only.' I was also granted a much higher code word clearance, which gave me access to the most sensitive signals intelligence that needed decrypting only for the captain's eyes.

It was a heavy responsibility that I took extremely seriously. But nothing could have prepared me for the crisis that unfolded just before one of our scheduled departures.

In the days leading up to our patrol, the signal traffic became increasingly agitated, suggesting we needed to get out to sea as soon as possible. But then came an engineering report that stopped us all in our tracks. A severe crack had developed in a pipe called the 'trouser leg,' which carried steam from the reactor to the turbines that powered the boat.

If that crack were to worsen, it would be catastrophic. We would lose the ability to cool the reactor, leading to a meltdown that could vaporize the submarine and everyone on board. It was the nightmare scenario that every submariner dreaded, and the consensus among the engineering team was clear—we should not, under any circumstances, be put to sea in our current condition.

But the political pressures were immense. The prime minister and the Admiralty were adamant that we could not afford to have a gap in our deterrent coverage. And so, despite the grave risks, the order came down to sail anyway.

I remember feeling a sense of unreality as we prepared to cast off lines and head out to sea. It was as if I was on autopilot, going through the motions of my job while my mind reeled with the knowledge of the ticking time bomb that lay beneath all of our feet.

At the last minute, as the current 'officer of the day,' I was dispatched to the stores at HMS Neptune to fetch a part that was stopping us from sailing, only to be told by a surly clerk that he couldn't possibly release it to me.

'Yes, sir, we've got one in stock,' he smirked. 'But if I give you that, I won't have one. It's Polaris-only stock, you see— only for emergencies.'

I felt my temper flare. 'You little shit,' I growled. 'You're stopping a Polaris submarine from going to sea. Do you have any idea what that means?'

In the end, it took the intervention of Commodore Clyde himself, who personally carried the part down to the boat, to get us the vital component we needed. I suspect the clerk in the store was never seen again!

Off we sailed. The mood on board was grim, with a palpable sense of fear and unease permeating every compartment. To make matters worse, our original eight-week patrol was soon extended to ten weeks. Then to 12, and finally 14-and-a-half long, stress-filled weeks beneath the waves.

We were instructed to keep our speed down, maintaining a steady four knots to minimise the strain on the damaged pipe. The engineers worked around the clock to monitor the crack, terrified that even the slightest deviation in pressure could cause it to split wide open.

The psychological toll was immense. Tempers frayed, and fights broke out over the slightest provocations. One man, driven half-mad by the unrelenting stress and claustrophobia, even tried to open the escape hatch while we were at depth— a move that would have doomed us all in an instant.

In a moment of grim practicality, the captain ordered us to let the man be. 'He'd need the strength of King Kong to crack that seal,' he said quietly as we watched the would-be escapee strain and heave against the immovable hatch. In the end, the man collapsed from exhaustion and was strapped into his bunk, thrashing and screaming until he eventually calmed.

But even amid such darkness, we found some moments of joy. Someone organised a makeshift golf tournament, setting up 'holes' that ran the boat's length—from the torpedo room, past the reactor compartment, through the mess and the bunk spaces. The tension lifted for a few precious hours as we laughed, joked and bet on who would sink the most unlikely putts.

The trouser leg incident reminds of me another issue we submariners faced, which needs a little technical explanation, but represented a huge danger to us crew members. It is not without controversy.

The maximum design accident (MDA), also known as the maximum credible accident, is a concept used in the design and safety assessment of nuclear-powered submarines. It refers to the most severe accident scenario that the submarine can encounter.

The MDA is a major failure of the reactor operating system, its associated cooling system, and one of many other critical systems that support its safety, such as reactor malfunctions, loss of coolant accidents, collisions, and many other disasters that a submarine can encounter during its operational life.

An MDA can be caused by human error where the people controlling the reactor plant make a mistake. There could also be a design defect, when a part of the nuclear power plant onboard a nuclear submarine is either designed badly or possibly made with weaker and less expensive materials. There could also be sabotage.

Another factor could be the use of the wrong or cheap alternatives for any part of the submarine. These fall into a number of separate failure zones. Cheap steel, wood, aluminium, rubber seals, poor welding using cheap equipment and components of the welds.

If any of the above occurred, the systems could degrade very quickly when under great pressure or overuse in events such as a very fast underwater transit; do not forget that a submarine can operate at twice the speed submerged than it can on the surface.

In nuclear-powered submarines, the MDA typically focuses on reactor safety and the ability to prevent or mitigate a nuclear reactor accident. This includes scenarios such as control rod malfunctions, loss of coolant accidents, and reactor scram.

Inside the submarine's nuclear power plant, the nuclear reactor
and the equipment contains and controls the chain reactions, most commonly fuelled by uranium-235, to produce heat through fission. The heat warms the reactor's cooling agent, typically water, to produce steam. The steam is then channelled to spin turbines, activating an electric generator to create low-carbon electricity.

From this, we produce our own electricity for all of the submarine's secondary services such as warm water to shower in or a light on your bunk where you can read before going to sleep

Given the many potential risks and faults that can take place on a submarine, it's no exaggeration to say that the British Government is guilty of knowingly putting the lives of thousands of submariners at risk of radiation poisoning. They knew about problems with the reactor and the huge doses of radiation that the sailors onboard were receiving but denied the crews of these submarines would most likely suffer from problems later on in life.

Crews were not allowed to wear a dosimeter or radiation tracker of any form. We were never informed of the danger they were putting themselves in by not being told these radiation levels (this could be a major data protection breach). As a result, submariners' life expectancy is less than the general public.

*

Finally, back on dry land, I managed to finally relax, although a different form of disaster awaited me. I was playing a game of squash with the captain—a rare privilege—and it ended in catastrophe when I snapped my Achilles tendon while lunging for a difficult shot.

'What's up, old boy?' the captain asked as I writhed on the court, clutching my leg in agony.

'I'll go and get you some help,' he said, disappearing up for a moment. A few minutes later, he returned with a lighter, a pack of cigarettes, and a pint of beer.

'Sorry, Andrew,' he said with a rueful grin. 'Best I could do under the circumstances.'

I ended up being airlifted to an RAF base hospital, where the doctors told me I would be out of action for at least six months. However, I was determined not to let my injury keep me from my duties or crewmates. I pushed myself through an intense rehab regimen, gritting my teeth against the pain as I forced my wounded leg to bear weight, then to walk, then to run.

In the end, I rejoined Repulse just six weeks after the incident. My wife at the time was less than thrilled—she knew that, given the choice, I would always choose the camaraderie of my fellow submariners over the comforts of hearth and home.

But that is the essence of what it means to serve beneath the waves. It's a life that sometimes demands everything of you—your time, energy and sanity. But it also gives you something in return—a sense of purpose, of belonging to something greater than yourself.

As I look back on those days now, with the benefit of hindsight and the wisdom of age, I am struck by the incredible resilience and fortitude of the men I served with. We faced challenges that would have broken lesser crews, and we did it with a mixture of grim determination and gallows humour that sustained us through the darkest of times.

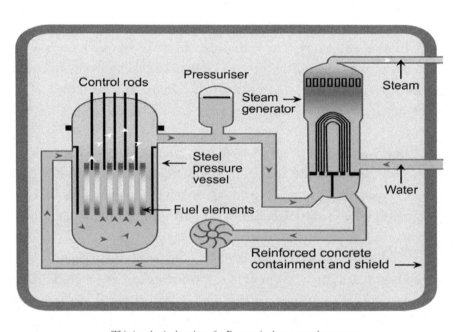

This is a basic drawing of a Rressureised water nuclear reactor.

10. FINAL YEARS

L eaving the submarine service was one of the hardest moments of my life. The Navy had been my home, family and identity for so long that I wasn't sure who I was without it. The ending was not of my choosing, although I managed to spend a few more years supporting the Navy in a desk job.

My final submarine was HMS Upholder, where I was an additional officer brought on board to complete my training as a submarine officer of the watch (dived). I joined her while she was in the final stages of being built in Barrow-in-Furness, about eight weeks away from sailing to undertake the first exercise of a new submarine—the deep dive.

Upon completing the deep dive, the captain wanted to spend two more weeks training the crew in emergency procedures at sea. This required every crew member to know every vital valve to shut, the door to operate, where the emergency stations were, and the correct procedures to make the submarine safe. We did this in preparation for the upcoming workup by the Captain Submarine Sea Training (CSST) staff.

We completed the deep dive and surfaced, but the rough weather prevented us from disembarking the pilot who had guided us out of the shallow waters of Barrow. So, we sailed north to the submarine base at Faslane near Helensburgh in

Scotland, where I continued my training while waiting for the day we were due to sail for the workup.

At this point, I was already qualified as an ocean navigator, officer of the watch (surfaced), and frigate and submarine navigation officer. When we worked with Special Forces like the SAS, SBS or Royal Marines, they would come on board and take over the torpedo shop. They didn't socialise much with the crew and would often surface in the middle of the night. They had a different aura about them—steel in their eyes, a breed apart.

On the morning of our departure for the first phase of CSST, I left my accommodation in the officers' mess ashore and walked down to the boat around 5 a.m. We were scheduled to sail at 10 a.m. after embarking on the sea training staff. To my surprise, I found the navigator standing on the submarine's casing by the rudder. When I asked him how he was, he replied that he'd had better days.

Concerned, I inquired about the problem, and he informed me that he had failed to make any preparations for our departure. Literally no charts were made up for the next four weeks of our operational sea training. I was speechless at first, then blurted out, 'You are fucking joking?' But sadly he wasn't. The man had clearly lost the plot. He walked past me and went below, leaving me contemplating what would happen next.

'Lieutenant Butterfield, report to the Captain,' came the order. 'How long is it going to take you to make the charts to get us out of here?' the Captain asked.

'A few hours, just to get us to deep water,' I replied.

'Do not expect to get any sleep in the next two weeks, and don't expect any credit,' he said grimly.

Our sailing was delayed by 24 hours, but I needed a quiet, undisturbed space to work. Food and water were delivered to me, along with a bucket for relieving myself. They put me in the 'sims and gyro' room, where I placed a board over the huge compasses and fetched the needed charts. There were hundreds of signals I needed to check. I virtually lived down there for about a few weeks, occasionally sleeping due to exhaustion.

We sailed for another operation from Faslane in February, knowing that the weather forecast was awful. We would be sailing into gale-force winds and a very dangerous place—the transit of the North Channel, the body of water that connects the Irish Sea to the Atlantic. The danger here was fourfold: wind speed, sea height, tidal streams and tidal rips.

At this point, I was not the navigator but undertook my duties as an officer of the watch (surfaced) and an officer of the watch (dived), though under supervision for the latter. It was made clear to the officers on board that we would hit extreme weather with gale-force winds and high seas, which we were sailing directly into.

I started my watch and proceeded to the bridge to take over as the officer of the watch (surfaced). We couldn't dive because we didn't have the authority from the Navy Command, as no dived water was available. Going up the conning tower from inside the boat, I got soaked—it was like climbing up inside a very strong shower. Eventually, I made it to the top of the bridge and had the quickest handover I think I've ever had. Then, my lookout and I were left to it.

The sea became wilder, and the winds were blowing at gale force 9-12. We were in trouble. After being battered by a number of these giant waves, I asked the captain if, for safety reasons, I could clear the bridge and come below to complete the watch on the periscope, as I could see nothing at all in the awful weather conditions from my position on the bridge. To my complete surprise, he said no, called me an idiot, and accused me of being incapable of doing my duties on the bridge. I asked him three more times over the next 30 minutes and got the same answer each time.

About an hour later, we hit a massive wave. I was thrown to the back of the bridge, and my back was partially fractured. Ignoring the pain, I cleared the bridge, helping the lookout back down into the conning tower. I then shut the lids on the top of the bridge and got below.

On arrival in the control room, the captain growled something at me, and I left his cabin and retired to my bunk. I got out of my soaked gear and into my rack, where I slept until the adrenaline wore off, and I woke up in extreme pain.

I was later told that I had probably saved the lookout's life and myself. I don't know. All I do know is that I was told never to tell what happened, which I haven't until now.

Today, I still have a fractured back, and the discs below the fracture have compressed over time, trapping the nerves, which is very painful. I have had to live with this pain 24 hours a day, seven days a week. My injury and my report of the incident were covered up, as there are no records of my report or the injuries. Had this been reported through official channels, I would have received better treatment and possibly some compensation, which I haven't claimed. I may have been able to lead a better life.

Doctors and neurosurgeons have now classified me as disabled. I cannot walk more than 10-15 paces without being breathless. I used to be a good squash player, runner and swimmer, but now I cannot exercise, which is heartbreaking as it was a massive part of my life.

The submarine service shaped me profoundly, both good and bad, and will always be a defining part of my life story. By sharing my experiences, I hope to honour the memory of those I served with and shed some light on a part of history that often remains in the shadows.

After leaving the submarines, I took on a desk job where I started building a relational database to manage Navy personnel—pay, pension, recruitment, retention, forecasts, etc. It was a better system for reporting more effectively.

I was promoted to Lieutenant Commander, and I took over a project that had been failing. I carved it into manageable tasks, approved the budget, and delivered it all. It changed how the Navy recruited and the kind of people they sought.

I rebuilt another database that allowed Admiral Boyce to examine big numbers and determine what he needed to do. He was delighted with the results.

The Navy helped me retrain in IT, shaping my second career. I spent six weeks on a course paid for by the Navy (resettlement training) and earned a chartered management qualification, plus some other management-focused certifications. I was ready to walk out into the 'real world.'

Looking back, I realise that my time in the Navy, particularly in the submarine service, had an immense impact on my life. It taught me the value of discipline, teamwork and perseverance in adversity. It showed me the depths of my resilience and the strength of the bonds that can form between people who face extreme challenges together.

But it also left its scars, both physical and emotional. The injury I sustained on that fateful day on HMS Upholder has been a constant companion, a reminder of the sacrifices we make to serve our country. And the psychological toll of living and working in such a high-pressure, high-stakes environment is not easily shaken off.

As I embarked on my new career in the civilian world, I carried these experiences with me. The skills I had learned in the Navy—leadership, problem-solving and the ability to remain calm under pressure—served me well in my new role. But I also had to learn to adapt to a different pace of life and a different set of expectations and priorities.

It wasn't always easy. There were times when I missed the adrenaline rush of submarine operations, the sense of purpose and camaraderie that came with being part of something greater than myself. But I also came to appreciate the simple joys of a life lived at a slower pace—time with family and friends and the freedom to pursue my interests and passions.

And through it all, I never lost my connection to the sea, to the silent world beneath the waves that had shaped me in such profound ways. Even now, years later, I find myself drawn to the ocean's edge, gazing out at the horizon and remembering the adventures and challenges of my youth.

In the end, I suppose that's the true legacy of my time in the submarine service. Not the medals or the accolades, but the memories and the lessons learned, the friendships forged in the crucible of shared adversity. These things stay with us, shape us and define us long after we've hung up our uniforms and moved on to new chapters in our lives.

And so, as I look back on my journey from raw recruit to seasoned submariner to civilian once more, I do so with a sense of gratitude and pride. I am grateful for the opportunities I was given and for the people who believed in me and pushed me to be my best self. I am proud that I served my country with honour and distinction and was part of something greater than myself.

The submarine service will always be a part of who I am, a touchstone in my life's story. While the ending may not have been of my choosing, I know that the lessons I learned and the memories I made will always stay with me, guiding me through whatever challenges and adventures lie ahead.

Therefore, I am a submariner, now and forever, which is a bond that can never be broken, a legacy that will endure long after I am gone. It is the essence of who I am, and I would not trade it for anything.

Second Sea Lord and
Commander-in-Chief
Naval Home Command
Ministry of Defence
Victory Building
HM Naval Base
Portsmouth PO1 3LS
Telephone 01705-727005
PY 27005

2SL/CNH 720/4/1

Lieutenant Commander A E Butterfield Royal Navy
2 Coriander Way
Woodhall Park
Haydon Wick
Swindon
Wiltshire
SN2 2RZ

26 April 1996

Dear Andy,

Formal approval has now been given to your being placed on the Retired List of the Royal Navy on 27 May 1996 under the terms of the Defence Council Instruction for the Royal Navy No. 2/95. Your retirement under these circumstances does not, of course, in any way diminish all you have put into the Royal Navy and, to mark the occasion of your leaving the Active List, I am writing on behalf of the Secretary of State for Defence to convey to you Her Majesty The Queen's thanks for your service.

To Her Majesty's thanks I should like to add my own and that of my colleagues on the Admiralty Board, and we wish you every success and happiness for the future.

yours sincerely

Michael Boyce

Painting by David Brackman presented by H.M.S. *Upholder* to
Her Royal Highness The Duchess of Kent on the occasion of the commissioning of
H.M.S. *Upholder* 9th June, 1990.

Printed by
Borg Kenward & Co. Ltd
© 1990 Cornwall

*This is a postcard painted for commissioning of HMS Upholder. Each officer
onboard was presented with a framed print.*

*Opposite: This letter from Admiral Boyce was recieved with great thanks to
a wonderful boss. He confirmed my rank as Lt Commander*

The Crew of HMS repulse were all offered the opportuntiy to buy this, I did but now do not know what to do with it.

NOTES ON THE DEEP-SUBMERGENCE RESCUE VEHICLE (DSRV) AND THE LR5

Response to a cry for help

When a submarine accident occurs, time is of the essence. The survival of the crew depends on how quickly a rescue operation can be launched. That is why deep submergence rescue vehicles (DSRVs) are designed for rapid deployment in various scenarios. They can be transported by different means, such as:

- Truck: a DSRV can be loaded on a trailer and driven to the nearest port or airfield.
- Aircraft: a DSRV can be airlifted by a large cargo plane and dropped by parachute into the water.
- Ship: a DSRV can be carried by a surface vessel and launched by a crane or davit.
- Submarine: a DSRV can be attached to a specially configured Nuclear Submarine and released near the accident site.

Search and Rescue

Once a DSRV reaches the vicinity of the disabled submarine, it begins a search and rescue operation. The DSRV is equipped with sonar, lights, cameras and communication systems to locate and contact the stranded crew. The DSRV manoeuvres to the escape hatch of the submarine and establishes a watertight seal. Up to 24 personnel can be transferred from the submarine to the DSRV at a time. The DSRV then detaches from the submarine and ascends to the surface, where it can rendezvous with the mother ship or submarine. This process is repeated until all survivors are rescued.

Depth Capability

DSRVs are designed to operate at depths that exceed the limits of conventional diving. The pressure hull of a DSRV is made of high-strength steel or titanium, which can withstand immense water pressure at great depths. The DSRV also has thrusters, ballast tanks, and stabilisers to control its depth and attitude. The typical depth capability of a DSRV is less than 610 metres (approximately 2,000 feet), which covers most of the submarine operating areas. However, some DSRVs can reach depths of up to 1,524 metres (5,000 feet), which allows them to rescue submariners from deeper accidents.

Deployment

The following pages in this chapter show the actual deployment of a DSRV from the USA to the UK, and its progress as it moves from air to land and finally to sea on the

Mother Sub, which then takes the vehicle to the submarine in distress.

What goes in must come out and here it is on british soil after a long journey from the USA.

Opposite: The DSRV arriving at a Scottish airport.

The DSRV Loaded onto HMAV Ardennes for the next leg of its journey.

*Opposite: The DSRV being transported to port for onward transportation to
HMS Repulse.*

DSRV being loaded onto HMAV Ardennes.

Opposite: Off Loading the DSRV so it can begin its journey by road to a naval base where HMS Repulse awaits its arrival.

*On our way to demonstrate to the world that NATO maintains a strategic capability
to rescue distressed submariners.*

Opposite: The DSRV Being loaded onto HMS Repulse

The DSRV on the road.

Opposite: Its Scotland, different weather different days, all beautiful though.

DSRV being carefully lowered onto HMS Repulse

Opposite: The DSRV on the road from the airport to the Naval Base

An other shot of Mystic, This submersible has been used to rescue people for exercise and for maybe for real.

Opposite: Loading the DSRV onto HMS Repulse, a very delicate operation.

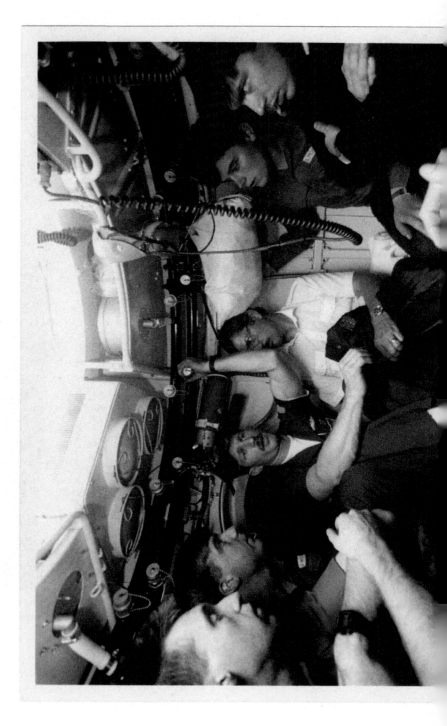

*This shows the cockpit of the DSRV where the two pilots sit and control
the submersible, once underwater.*

Opposite: This was a bit tight 15 people squashed in the DSRV, I was one of them.

The LR5 gently lowered into the Ocean to start its underwater search for the submarine in distress.

Opposite: This shows the British version of the DSRV. The LR5, here it is being deployed from a ship.

EPILOGUE

I have come to the end of this book, which has been a labour of love in my telling of my life in the Royal Navy and a tribute to the men and women who serve.

I wrote this book because I wanted to share my passion and admiration for the Royal Navy, in particular the Submarine Service, which has been a constant source of inspiration and guidance for me throughout my life.

I joined the Navy as a young man in 1977 and have never regretted my decision.

The Navy has given me the opportunity to travel the world, to learn new skills, to face difficult situations, and to make lifelong friends. It has also taught me the values of courage, commitment, discipline, and respect, which have shaped my character and my outlook on life.

The Royal Navy is not just a job, it is a way of life. It is a family that supports you, challenges you, and rewards you. It is a career that offers you variety, adventure, and satisfaction. It is a service that demands your loyalty, your professionalism, and your excellence. It is a force that protects our nation, our interests, and our allies. It is a legacy that you can be proud of, and a future that you can shape.

I know that the Royal Navy is not for everyone and that it requires a lot of sacrifice and dedication. But I also know that it can be one of the most rewarding and fulfilling choices you can make. If you are a young person who is looking for a challenge, a purpose, and a difference, I urge you to consider a career in the Royal Navy. You will not only serve your country, but you will also serve yourself. You will discover your potential, your passion, and your pride. You will become part of a team, a community, and a history. You will make a difference, not only to yourself but to the world.

Thank you for reading this book, and thank you for your interest in the Royal Navy Submarine Service. I hope that I have given you a glimpse of what it means to be a Submariner, and what it takes to be one. I hope that I have inspired you, informed you, and entertained you. And I hope that I have made you proud of our Royal Navy, as I am proud of it. It has been an honour and a privilege to serve in it and to write about it. I hope that you will join me in saluting it, and in wishing it fair winds and following seas.

Myself, when I was truly happy.

The Ancient Arms of

Butterfield

My Sword, my French Teddy bear who I was given at birth, he is called Bear. The picture was taken when I was given him.

Opposite: My Family Crest of Arms

*I have Six Grandchildren, for whom this book is written. They know not me and I
not them. Maybe in the future who knows?*

Printed in Great Britain
by Amazon

55212195R00076